ALCHEMY: THE ART AND SCIENCE OF TRANSFORMING LEAD INTO GOLD.

WHY DO YOU NEED A BRIEF AND WHY DOES IT MATTER IF IT'S KILLER OR NOT?

Because if you can write a killer brief for yourself, you're much more likely to get what you want; and if you can write a killer brief for others, you'll always have a job. Killer briefs simplify the complicated; they inspire, not just inform; and they are the seed, water and sunshine for the creation of amazing things (and help us avoid dabbling among the mediocre ones).

There are many benefits to writing a brief in the first place: a brief can help clarify thoughts; it can be the springboard to rich thinking; it saves creative resources; it streamlines decision-making; and it is the touchstone that ultimately provides cohesion, understanding and collective accountability (in other words, it's the last place we all agreed).

It is not just an item on your to-do list, an arbitrary part of the process or a throw-away activity. The power of writing down what it is you're looking for in terms of how you want people to feel, and what you want them to do about it, is a deliberate act of creation. There are rules and guidelines and suggestions in here that I have found to yield great success when applied to a brief. There is a certain kind of magic that is called up when an opportunity is articulated in (killer) brief form.

After many years of helping creative companies and agencies create passion brands and fiscal success, I've come to realize that rallying around the concept of making a killer brief the platform for creative development often resolves 80% of their issues. That a brief doesn't kill spontaneity, it creates opportunity and that idea generation is really born of a focused catalyst: a clear sense of what we want to have happen and where the areas of heat are that will give us the greatest chances of success.

Many of my friends and colleagues who write briefs for a living have said that the ideas presented here have helped them tremendously. I submit that if even one idea resonates and makes its way into your briefs it can make a huge difference. My goal in this has always been to help people make beautiful and important things and to have way more fun in the process. My wish is that this book does that for you.

REMEMBER WHAT IT IS.

A brief is the first creative step. With it, you should take a stand, not put forward only irrefutable facts or restate the obvious. It is both creative and brief. It is a bridge, if you will, between what is and what could be. It is a roadmap. A springboard for inspiration. A view of the brand through the eyes of a poet and an optimist. A snapshot of the human condition we can improve.

AND WHAT IT'S NOT.

It does not tell your creative team what to paint, why they should paint it or what colors to use. It highlights what part of the canvas the artist might want to start on. It is not a job order, a record of how much you know or how much work you've done. It is not a list of facts. It is a story. The first creative idea put forward. The best area of heat you have.

BRIEFS ARE A SPRINGBOARD FOR IDEATION.

Many companies use briefs internally (developers and designers need to find a common ground) and externally (companies give briefs to their agencies and web designers as an efficient way to share information and parameters for creation).

Briefs should be the first creative idea. They often serve as the 'last place we all agreed' prior to moving to creative development, and can help evaluate ideas in a strategic way and avoid personal preference to creep into what gets produced and what ends up on the cutting room floor.

When used correctly, briefs can help maintain consistency within a brand when several internal departments and/or suppliers are in play.

A BAD BRIEF INHIBITS IDEATION, A KILLER BRIEF INSPIRES IT.

Being able to write a killer brief is a life skill. Learning to write one begins with believing they are important, thinking differently about brands and engaging your poetic mind (vs. your strictly logical one). Note that the briefing is as important as the brief, but that one page document (yes, one page) can be the difference between having an impact and having valuable information sit on a shelf.

Briefs help with efficiency by saving creative resources. They help effectiveness by making sure everyone is on the same page. They streamline decision-making processes and articulate elements of a brand that can get lost in translation.

“A BRIEF IS ON
TRANSFORMA
CAN CREATE.”

E OF THE MOST
IVE PIECES WE

“A single moment of human emotion is enough to create a masterpiece.”

Margaret Sackville

CULTIVATE A CREATIVE MINDSET

While the creative brief form gives structure and discipline to this endeavor, the magic is not in the form – it's in the thinking that goes into filling it out. So with that in mind, it's critical to get in the right headspace before we start to answer the questions in the brief. I find that the enemies of creative thinking are all around us – we have less time then ever to just mull and we spend an inordinate amount of time in front of a computer, and often in PowerPoint, which (negatively) affects our creative thoughts and communications.

While we are all born creative, our realities let this muscle atrophy. We need to exercise that muscle – to let ideas flow through us – in order to become aware of the brilliant ones that bubble up. Here are a few ways to open the door to reconnecting with your creative thinking:

First, audit when and where you work best. Most of us do different kinds of tasks better at different times of day. For example, I write well in the morning (or evening with a glass of wine), but have a hard time during the day, which is usually interspersed with meetings.

Trying to think about and write a brief in front of a computer is next to impossible for most people I know - but writing a brief longhand in a place where you can borrow energy (a hotel lobby, quiet restaurant patio, etc), with an inspiring pen and paper, can make an immense difference.

Doing different work on different days can also make a huge impact. Once I snap into 'meeting mode,' I inevitably snap out of 'thinking/writing/creating' mode. So I pack all my meetings into a day and don't schedule any on another. Or I don't schedule anything until 10:30 so I have a block of uninterrupted time to finish creating before jumping into a different headspace. Whole companies have built cultures around 'defragging' the calendar and I find it's a small change that can reap grand rewards.

There are many other habits and exercises that help foster a creative headspace, but since this is about Killer Briefs, I'll ask you to look for those ideas in my book about Igniting Momentum.

“The difference between the right word and the almost right word is the difference between lightning and a lightning bug.”

Mark Twain

IN THE LAND OF GETTING EVERYONE ON THE SAME PROVERBIAL PAGE, THIS IS THE PAGE.

Once we know what we want to build, we need to design the blueprint for the 'architects' (your creative team, even if this is you). It's about getting clarity by putting words to it. The rest of this book will help you fill these out in the best possible way, but these are the questions we need to answer:

WHAT ARE WE SELLING?

What is our product or category? What are our 'units of sale?' That is, what is the physical output that provides the value they're 'paying' for? We are 'really' selling an emotional benefit, but endeavors such as these must be monetized to succeed. This question helps keep everyone focused on 'feeding the (business) machine.' Is it a sweater, a trip, a visit? What is the THING we are selling at the very core of this endeavor?

WHAT IS THE ASSIGNMENT?

What are we physically building with this brief (in terms of the output/deliverable: a website, an ad or campaign, a logo, a tagline, a brochure, etc.)? When I review briefs for agencies, this is often a glaring omission...the creative team begins struggling with what the parameters are for their ideas in terms of form and budget, which is a waste of time and energy. Be clear about the expectation and then help them to rock it.

WHY ARE WE DOING IT?

This is where we bring forward how we will define success. We must think about ideal effects beyond the obvious of adding value and increasing awareness. These are givens. Yes, we are selling something but what else? Do we need to inspire, convince, validate? Instill hope or nudge their fears in order to get them to act? We must keep an eye to differentiating but in the spirit of inviting preference and loyalty. We have to be clear about what we want them to do: Visit us? Buy online?

Once you figure out what you want to have happen you need to set a measurable goal. Measure what you can, even if you have to work backwards, because it sets client/team expectations (and allows for conversations about unrealistic ones early in the game). It frames the size of the task (is this an evolution or revolution?) and it creates momentum (what gets measured gets done, right?). At the back end it also helps create a case study for the work done because you captured a benchmark and agreed to measure the impact. You might think this is an add-on, but it’s a core driver to creating efficient and effective work.

WHO ARE WE TALKING TO?

Who are our cultists (high income customers who are enthusiasts) and low-hanging fruit (people who should be our lions but aren't) in terms of their shared behaviors and beliefs? They should already be a car shopper, chicken buyer, mango lover, beer drinker, etc. How do they live and what's important to them? This sentence should start with 'People who...' Please don't put demographics in here – I've yet to find them helpful. You're speaking to a shared mindset – the common threads across your audiences that makes them tick – and includes an element of why they care about what you have to offer. For example, Miller High Life is not really about the beer. It's about what MHL drinkers believe the brand stands for and the tribal beliefs they share with other MHL drinkers.

What is it about these people that makes our brand promise work? If we've done our job in talking to them, this should come fairly easily. If we're guessing, then be sure to focus on *what's in it for them not what we want to tell them about us.*

WHAT DO THEY CURRENTLY THINK?

Once you know who you are talking to, then you need to clearly outline what they believe that drives their behavior (toward us or away from us). What are the motivators and barriers that we need to address? What do they love about us/our product and/or category? Note: whoever says it first, loudest or best can own it even if it's true of all players. What is going on in their minds THE MOMENT our brand/category becomes more important and relevant to them than any other time in their day/year/lives? What is the problem we're helping them solve or the dream we're helping them reach?

WHAT DO THEY NEED TO THINK?

Or better yet, what do we need them to think in order to act the way we wish? Persuasion requires that a belief precedes a behavior. So what's that belief? What will be powerful enough to motivate them? Amplify what they currently think? Change what they think to overcome an obstacle? Either might work.

Contextually, the promise must bridge what they currently think and what we need them to think. I often get the promise and this section mixed up when writing – it's just how it comes out of me – but now that I know it, I write as much as I can think of for this question and then mine it for phrases that may work better being said out loud (as our promise) rather than in their heads (as a belief).

It may be as superficial as having them believe, 'wow, that's cool,' in order for them to buy it (or buy into it) but our promise must capture what our product or brand does for them and says about them to work optimally.

WHAT'S OUR PROMISE?

In other words, what is a slogan for the idea? In seven words or fewer. In fact, fewer is better. What will we do for them? Say about them? What will motivate them to believe us? I like to think of this line as the first (bad) tagline. I think of it as a bad tagline to take the pressure off and to not totally piss off the creative team. A tagline because it should be able to go on a t-shirt or bumper sticker that our tribe would wear proudly (and agree with). We should be able to put this line under a photo of our product and have it run as a billboard (thus, the seven words). It's not a directive, it's the first creative place to play and it should do the heavy lifting of the brief.

If you nail nothing else, nail this. It is what will keep the idea swirling and become the touchstone for reviewing creative to assess whether it's 'right' (as opposed to more subjective, evolving criteria). Getting this right and getting people aligned on this is what prevents do-overs. So worth it.

It doesn't have to make total sense on its own (without context of the briefing), but it should capture the essence of what we came to understand through the briefing. For example, Nikegoddess' 'Bring out the light within' is cryptic. It doesn't stand on its own. But it made my (all male) creative team pay attention long enough to answer their primary question: 'What the fuck is she talking about?' The balance here is that you need to tell them what you learned. And 80% of it will be what they already know (if they've been working on the account for awhile), but that is required for them to believe the other 20%. And sometimes you need to tickle their curiosity a bit to get them to want to unwrap a new 20%. That's what loaded language does. Once they understood that the 'light' is a confidence that shines from a woman when she's feeling strong and beautiful (which was our brand's new mission — to facilitate rather than be a standard to live up to), they could grasp the emotional benefit to our tribe of what we needed to do.

EXAMPLES:

MILLER HIGH LIFE | "Symbol of a real man."

AMTRAK | "Give yourself your undivided attention."

WP ZOO | "Reconnect with your creaturehood."

UMPQUA | "Refreshingly different."

COFFEE PEOPLE | "Local flavor."

OUTWARD BOUND | "Courage for life. "

NIKEGODDESS | "Brings out the light within."

WIDMER HEF | "The original wheat beer."

WHY SHOULD THEY BELIEVE US?

What relevant evidence or rationale supports this idea? It doesn't have to be a ton of irrefutable evidence, but it has to be sincere and convincing. It can be anecdotal vs. factual/literal – just be prepared to fight for it. You are getting people to fall in love with an idea – this is where we get them to believe that this idea just might work. If I don't know where else to start, I often start with this section and list out everything I think is important and then ladder up to make the brief fit this list.

Everything in the brief is fair game for the creative team. Just be sure to not throw in everything but the kitchen sink – it should be a curated list of product features, testimonials, satisfaction scores, etc., that helps tell this story.

You may also want to think of this section as 'cocktail party fodder' – things you'd want to tell someone if you had their undivided attention and they wanted to know about what you're selling.

WHAT IS OUR PERSONALITY?

Every great brand has a personality — whether defined by a physical style (Apple) or a voice (Mini Cooper). In my world, brands must have a defined voice — a personality — that keeps them from becoming fragmented (or schizophrenic). This voice is defined by using three words (active, personality-based adjectives that could describe a person).

Integrity doesn't work within this definition because it must be demonstrated via actions and is, in my view, a given. So what three words would people use to describe your brand currently? What three words (same or different) would you ideally want them to use? This exercise alone can help clarify what your work needs to do. If you can get your team aligned on these three ideal words, move to a poster child (a physical example of these words brought to life in the real world). For example, a poster child for 'creative, youthful, sophisticated' could be Absolut; 'confident, worldly, real' may be closer to Susan Sarandon than Kathy Lee Gifford. Comparisons work, too — more this than that. The objective is to have a touchstone for how the brand sounds and behaves. If we say we're more 'Jon Stewart than Jay Leno' you get an idea of where we live (and where we don't). Seek to stand apart authentically.

Another way to come at this is to think of your brand on a playground with other brands (if you can't play along here you may be in the wrong game). In this case, who would we want our brand to play with? If we can define our tribe (two or three brands we relate to or look up to), then we can back out the qualities they have. If you're stuck, try listing words that you DON'T want. For example, Umpqua Bank looked to Virgin as their poster child, not another bank. We backed personality out of this realization (since they were new and didn't yet have a personality it was the best way to go). Their North Star was their 'revolution.' What characteristics does a 'revolutionary' brand have? It's your job to define this space.

REMEMBER: YOU GET THREE WORDS THAT BECOME CORNERSTONES FOR ALL YOU DO AND SAY AND THEY DON'T CHANGE.

EVER.

BE BOTH CREATIVE AND BRIEF

A brief should be the expression of your best idea (what you would do if it was your money), and the summary of every important thought. It should not be longer than a single sheet of paper.

What happens if you have multiple products and/or audiences? Whatever you do, don't put everything in one brief. Each OUTPUT deserves its own brief, but it's important to find the common thread between all of them.

Whatever your situation, you need to focus on writing the Mother Brief first, which is the main expression of the brand's intention. For example, Nike's Mother Brief would ideally inspire the overarching concept around 'Just Do It', while individual briefs would be written for individual sports (Golf, Basketball, etc.) as well as individual outputs for each of these business units. Virgin is another example: The Mother Brief may hover around the idea of 'revolution' but individual briefs cover the various business units (mobile, music, space travel, etc.)

Do NOT include the client history beyond the reason for wanting this output (the objective) in the brief. Most of the troublesome briefs I've looked at spend way too much time telling the history of the account and way too little time telling the creative team how they could collectively solve the problem. You can speak to the history/background easily in the briefing (where it's way more powerful). You want your creative team to be able to pull this one page off and hang onto it – and focus on the sparks of what needs to get done and why people will care.

This bears repeating: ONE page is the springboard for ideation – it should be inspirational even more so than being informational. And if you can't get it to one page, you're trying to do too much.

“It is with words as with sunbeams. The more they are condensed, the deeper they burn.”

Robert Southey

DOES IT MAKE YOUR TOES CURL?

The seven words (or fewer) that form your main idea are the heart and soul of the brief. This one line will haunt recipients of the brief in hallways, in the car, in the shower — where the magic of ideation happens.

It should be loaded — which means it should not be dry or boring, but invite people to raise an eyebrow (or two) and want more information, explanation or context.

These main thoughts or promises are not intended to be externally-facing, but could be. Ideally the agency can 'plus them' (for example, Widmer Hef's positioning line started as "The original wheat beer" in the brief but ended up as "America's Original Wheat Beer" and is better from both a legal standpoint and a positioning standpoint). This line doesn't have to pass the test of being ready for prime time, but it should be a worthy placeholder for the 'sign off' of all creative being developed, which should hang together under this umbrella. If it's too narrow, make your dots bigger (pull up to something higher level that allows for some campaign legs but doesn't give up what's right because it's a little hard). This is the fine line within creative development and deserves more attention than it's getting here, but best to start with having a point of view that isn't easy to forget or ignore (aka, inspires them insidiously in quiet moments).

The tests it must pass at this point are:

The 'space between test' – does it capture the magic intersection of what we as a company love and what our best customers love?

The 'mom test'– could you say it to your mom and she'd get the basic idea?

The 'elevator test' – can you explain it in an elevator ride? By the way, this is much harder to do in the NW because of our short buildings, but maybe that's what fuels us.

The 'crinkle test' – can you say it out loud without crinkling your nose?

The 'dog test' – this isn't really a test but it is my dog's primary job to listen to all the possible 'main messages' without judgement. He rules at this.

"If you can't explain it to a six year old, you don't understand it yourself."

Albert Einstein

REMEMBER THE CREATIVE TEAM IS YOUR AUDIENCE

Even though the client has to approve the brief, the purpose of the brief is to inspire ideation and creation. Therefore, the audience is the creative team, or those who charge forth to find ideas to answer what the brief is asking for. The client should agree to the intent of the brief, not wordsmith it. It should inspire your creative team as opposed to telling them what to do, it should inform possibilities and encourage conversations that start with 'What if?' or 'Why not?'.

Stan Richards wisely told me at the start of my career that, "If you are of value to the creative department, you will always have a job." I asked what was of value and he told me to ask them (all) and I still start here.

Thanks, Stan.

GIVE YOURSELF GOOSEBUMPS

Here's the rub: if you're writing the brief, you have been chosen to go first. To crack the first creative nut by deciding where on the canvas to start. To catch vapor in a jar. And it may take nearly as much effort to get people to see what you see. They will not clap. Music will not play. They may not even get it. Even if it's utterly amazing. Two things are at play with this insight: 1. Don't rush to evaluate it and 2. Give yourself goosebumps. Not rushing to evaluate is the most difficult – for your team and for yourself. Great ideas have been left on the cutting room floor because 'the client would never buy it' when the client didn't even get to see it. Let it wash over you. Try it on like a coat for a day. See if you're thinking about it the next day (like a good movie). If it's wrong, put into words why it's wrong. And think of something more right. Then share.

Writing a killer brief (as opposed to stopping at a reasonably acceptable brief) will not have immediate rewards for most of you. And it may even make some people nervous. So the impetus has to come from an internal desire to do it for its own reward. To go until you've given yourself goosebumps and it's made you fall in love with the brand, the opportunity and ultimately, the project. It's about treating everything as though it is vitally important.

The Nikegoddess project didn't start out as such. It was actually a $10,000 video project to fire up the sales team for a seasonal initiative to try to stem the bleeding from the women's business. So we focused on our lions (women who buy lots of gear) and found out what we needed to do for them and what we needed to say about them. We wrote a brief and created a platform to sell the client on doing more. And they did. Nikegoddess as a brand was born. And led to an amazing site and relationship and new retail stores. At its height, it was the most profitable division within Nike. All from a seasonal initiative.

Giving yourself goosebumps is about doing it for love and honor. Yours. You must love it. You must believe in it. You must do it for yourself first and foremost (and for your portfolio). This gives you courage and focus — so you aren't sidetracked by what you think others will do or say. It's not about external validation (until results come in later).

BEWARE OF THE

RATIONAL SKEPTICAL MIND

While it may serve us to be the devil's advocate on occassion, it will only bring you down. Some of the greatest ideas in the world were thought insane.

Truth is, skeptics have never really been known for coming up with much of value. And as marketers, it's our job to see the beauty in things and to make others see it too.

So put your poet hat on when writing a brief and take some creative license. Figure out how to get people to fall in love by following what people currently love.

Remember that you can approach selling a pen by talking about how long the ink will last, or you can inspire people to use one by reminding them that it was the instrument that wrote the cure for cancer or the greatest love letter in the world.

It's your call.

REMEMBER WHAT YOU ARE REALLY SELLING

IT'S NOT WHAT YOU MAKE, IT'S WHAT YOU DO FOR THEM AND/OR SAY ABOUT THEM.

If our product is what we MAKE and physically sell, this is about what we do for them and/or say about them. Also known as a magnetic virtue, it's one word that sums up the emotional benefit to our customers. For example, Southwest Airlines makes cheap airline seats. This allows people to be spontaneous, which could also be described as a type of freedom. Southwest is really selling freedom; Volvo, safety and Westin, sanctuary.

Once you have this nailed, getting clarity and alignment on everything else becomes much, much easier. If you don't believe brands can be badges, consider that there are more Harley Davidson stickers on cars than there are Harley's on the road. People buy into the idea (and brand) even if they can't buy into the product literally.

KNOW WHERE THE FINE LINES ARE

As a brief writer, success lies in finding the fine line between bravery and stupidity, confidence and arrogance, genius and madness. You have more creative license than you think you do but don't abuse your power.

PAINT A PICTURE OF THE

AUDIENCE

AND MAKE THEM

LIKEABLE

Both who they are, what they do and what they believe. Their hopes, dreams, fears and desires. Why do they do what they do and believe what they believe? What drives their attitudes and behaviors? To know a man is to know what drives him, not what describes him. If you don't know, describe him by inference. For example, by where he might see the ad ("Rolling Stone readers").

Don't get bogged down in irrelevant details. Follow beliefs and behaviors. Make the creatives empathize and want to think about them. Think of how someone might describe you — what would tell them something important about how to talk to you? Is how much you make a critical element to understanding you? Think about it.

A Mindset Manifesto (like Apple's "Think Different" campaign) is a great way to nail your thinking around your audience (and a great addendum to a one page brief).

ANSWER THE

MINDSET

YOU WISH TO

AFFECT

This goes back to 'make it hang together.' The message must fit into their head space and it needs to touch what they want.

Your main message should address them as well as the brand. It should fill the space between what you and they share – like holding up a mirror to your best customers and tapping the collective love and what they love. It should be a payoff for the context you've created in the beginning of the brief. It should definitely be the bridge between what they currently think and what we want them to think. It needs to answer what we want them to do, which is tied to what we want to have happen. It's a tall order. It's a big deal. I find writing out possible lines and picturing them as a bumper sticker or the pay-off to our logo on a t-shirt helps me get closer. Say them out loud. Would your best customers agree with it? Care about it? Would your best staffers?

On top of connecting internal and external drivers (things people care deeply about), make sure your whole brief connects – that is, ensure each question/answer/place hangs together with the others. It must, overall, tell a cohesive story or bring to life a cohesive point of view. At the end of the day, be sure you've answered: 'What's in it for them?'

CONNECT THE
BIG JUICY DOTS

If it was easy, everyone would be doing it. I had a statistics professor once (and gleefully only once — and who, as an aside, had an accent that made the word 'statistics' sound like 'sadistics,' which still amuses me) who gave me a perspective that I think relates. He talked about troubleshooting the task of plotting a graph (think of each question on the brief as a data point that you're plotting). The purpose is to be able to look for trends or patterns across the whole. The problem was that most line up, but you'd have a crazy outlier. Or none would line up which would just be maddening. The trick, he would say, "was to make your dots bigger" — that is, go back to the data and 'pull up' to a higher order data point (or insight or benefit).

Remember, Southwest Airlines sells cheap airline seats and tickets (the product). Strong brands always speak to what's in it for their customers. Southwest laddered up to what they're really selling, which is spontaneity. With cheap seats, you can travel anytime, anywhere you wish. But spontaneity wasn't a big enough 'dot.' If you are able to be spontaneous, you are really free. So ultimately, cheap seats equate to traveler freedom. Freedom is a big dot. And a juicy one. One that people care about. Best to play there because it gives you many places to go (and can pull together many dots). Ladder up until it fits.

BE

LOADED

It’s pretty easy to write a brief that isn’t wrong, but it’s hard to write a brief that inspires you. A large part of it comes from the words you use to express your idea. For example, the zoo brief could have been "the zoo reminds you that you have something in common with the animals," but would not have been as impactful as "reconnect with your creaturehood."

Put it out there, especially if it raises eyebrows.

AVOID

CLIENT SPEAK

If clients could write a good brief, they probably would (and save the money). Remember that your job is to translate the client's (brand's) equities and situation into something that creatives can wrap their magic around. If you use the client's language, you run a very good risk of being accused (rightfully so) of 'drinking the kool-aid' and will likely be as involved (not) as the client.

One of the best ways to get around this, if at all possible, is to write the brief before having the full client briefing (initial thoughts are often the strongest). Barring that, have someone who doesn't work in your industry read the brief and throw out any words that have to be explained. We often forget that our job is to simplify a complicated problem rather than the other way around. Don't equate simplicity with stupidity.

Throw out jargon (anything your mom would need you to explain). Make it human. Allow for points of connection.

DON'T SAY WHAT

NEEDS

TO BE

DEMONSTRATED

We're often tempted (or coerced) into trying to make the message something it can't be...like the phrase "trust me." If you say it, the opposite becomes true. If the client wants to be thought of as progressive, trustworthy, etc., don't say these things, but find a way to demonstrate them and let the audience do the math. Find out what you need to say that *supports* an authentic truth (what they'll experience).

WRITE AT LEAST THREE

VERSIONS LONGHAND

There is something about longhand that opens the door to your creativity. And there's something about computers that tends to stifle it. It may be because as we're jotting a thought down, we get distracted by misspelling a word or that all the words tend to look the same. I think we're starting to think in powerpoint bullets instead of complete thoughts.

You can always type it up, but let your mind flow with a great pen. Give words personalities. Circle hot words and put them together in the next brief. Find the most critical sentences and thoughts and put them in a different section of the brief and see what happens.

Writing briefs longhand first (and rewriting them a few times) allows me to let my subconscious vent and play with the order of inspirational nuggets. It's a bit like putting a puzzle together – find what goes where in general terms and then start connecting smaller pieces.

TAKE THE TIME TO

LISTEN

TO YOUR

CUSTOMERS

If you've come to this point and are still not feeling it (clarity, goosebumps, etc.) that's almost to be expected. In all the years I've been writing briefs, the best, most impactful briefs have come from insights gleaned from actually talking to people. The beliefs they have that drive their behaviors, the emotions attached to them, their desires for what they want a brand to do for them and say about them — these are all areas of heat that create magic.

A few things to consider:

They will tell you everything if you do it right.

Not all customers are created equal.

It's about possibilities not proof.

It doesn't have to be expansive or intensive.

It needs to happen before the work is done and money has been spent (meaning do it upfront as opposed to 'testing it' afterward).

Qualitative RULES.

Guessing is really, really expensive.

I have yet to be able to guess what moves consumers, but once I see the world from their point of view, it makes total sense; then the whole team can get behind how we're going to do what we need to do. Talking to customers will also do a few great things for the creative development dynamic:

It creates a 'referee' that helps everyone get on the same page (and reduces circular conversations even more than the brief).

It changes the power dynamic (whoever has the most information about the target generally drives).

You're MUCH more likely to be able to hit the right person, at the right time, with the right message – that is, one that is meaningful and motivating – which will allow you to win big.

“It’s easy to make millions of dollars. You just find out what people want, and then give it to them.”

Yahoo Founder

THE RIGHT PEOPLE WILL GIVE YOU THE RIGHT INSIGHTS.

There is an art to doing creative research well, (which I plan to cover in another book) but, essentially, here is what provides me with the most success:

Be sure you have the right people in the room (I start with current customers who make up the lions' share of your revenue) and if you can observe them in situation, all the better.

—

Have five outstanding questions to ask them, then stop talking but don't leave the room until you understand where they're coming from. I like to think of the role of the moderator as one that is similar to a method actor: you need to put yourself in their shoes so you can answer questions on their behalf without asking them. This way you will find out what drives their beliefs and behaviors at a core level.

It’s best if you can see them even if you can’t be in the same room with them. Your job is to articulate what they meant as opposed to playing back what they said.

I take notes when interviewing people so they don’t feel like they’re put on the spot (when you’re looking straight at them) and I tend to remember more when I write down what I hear.

After the session is done, say everything out loud that you found interesting (even if it’s to your dog). You’ll know when you’ve found an insight because music will play. What I mean by this is pay attention to what ‘haunts’ you the next day (like thinking about a movie you saw the night before), or what you’re excited to talk about or what makes you more curious about what is going on.

I write everything down on a big (unlined) sheet of paper so I can pull back and look for connections and relationships between these ideas. Insights are not often served in a linear, logical fashion, but are pieces of a puzzle that you have to figure out where they live in the bigger picture. Having a sounding board (ideally the creative team) can help because they'll tell you what they found of interest while you're brain-dumping. Even those who don't work on your project can be helpful to see what you don't and they'll usually indulge you if you buy the beer.

IT'S NOT ABOUT PLAYING BACK WHAT THEY SAID, IT'S ABOUT BRINGING TO LIFE WHAT THEY *MEANT*.

DON'T ASK FOR PERMISSION, JUST DO IT.

If you meet resistance from the client or your internal team when pitching this plan, here are a couple of ways around it:

Talking to a few people doesn't have to take more than a day or two (the alternative is that you'll just have to make it up and ironically this takes longer and costs more).

Don't call it research, call it creative development and take the money out of that budget (and explain that it's required for you to do what you need to do well). Once you have a win, you're golden.

THINK OF IT AS
THEATER
NOT BATON-PASSING

The brief is only half the battle. The briefing is one of the greatest opportunities you have for creative development.

Here's what I find works best:

Make sure all electronics are turned off (they don't need to take notes).

Don't read it – tell a story. Bring pictures that help illustrate your audience or brand character (pulled out of magazines, for example) or show clips from movies – whatever will make the right impression and linger with them.

You can send the brief ahead of time, if you are comfortable. It gives them time to digest it before you chat and can give more time for fruitful conversations.

Take them out of the office – ideally, at the end of the day and over food and a beverage.

Make it relevant and inspiring: You are telling a story, highlighting a problem and selling the solution. The main thought must get them from 'what they currently think' to 'what we want them to think.' It all has to feel right in our hearts and guts – that it is what we need to say to get them to do what we want them to do. Period.

MOST IMPORTANTLY, HAVE FUN.

MAKE SURE YOU CAN

PROVIDE

SOME POSSIBLE

WAYS TO GO

One of the best ways to help them see what you see is to do the first bad ad.

It might be a great ad, but you don't want to piss them off at the outset (it's 'bad' because it's their job to make a good one, you just did this to help them see). If you can't come up with one or two examples of how your brief would translate to an ad, find an existing ad that delivers against a similar strategy. If still stuck, talk to people and ask them for ideas to walk into the briefing with. If still stuck, your team will likely be, too – talk to them about it off the record first, but plan to go back to the drawing board.

BE FLEXIBLE BUT STAY

TRUE

TO YOUR

CONVICTION

Tough place to be, but believe that creative guys were the first planners and some of them are quite good at it. Sometimes, in playing with it, you find a better way in or a more clarified (or different) problem. Or just a rockin' cool idea. Have the flexibility to go with a better idea, not just cave because it's hard or they don't have the time to think about your point of view. Remember, it may take clarification after the briefing and if you ask, they might let you in as long as you're helping and not judging.

BE PREPARED TO

EXPECT

THE

UNEXPECTED

When the creative is ready for review, it's essential that you remind everyone what you agreed to accomplish at the onset of the assignment (and it's really important that you keep this in mind when you see the work).

It's not about what you like or don't like or how well it matches what was in your head or what you expected to see. Great ideas, like a killer brief, do not have the benefit of music playing even when they're awesome. In fact, they should make you a bit uncomfortable because they're tapping something emotional or novel (ideally). Also, remember that creative work shouldn't lay things out like a 2x4, but rather have the audience 'do the math' so they end up thinking and feeling as we wish them to.

The framework I like to use here is 'Angel/Devil/Judge' — a bit more than a 'compliment sandwich' in that it should be genuine feedback mixed with questions about your sticking points.

Angel: Something you genuinely like about the approach, the idea, the language, etc. What you're really saying is, 'Please don't touch this bit when you go to revise.'

Devil: Your sticking points, ideally framed as a question: 'Why are we saying it in this way?' and 'Do we think they'll react negatively to this bit?'

Judge: Not an executional dictate, but a possible way to go. 'What if we…?', 'Could we think about doing…?' and 'What do you think about…?' This should be a gentle conversation as opposed to being prickly.

At the end, I defer to the creative wisdom of the team. Many a great idea has been killed before the client even got a chance to review it, so don't play it too safe.

One of the best pieces of advice I received around this topic was to plan ahead and create trust and language around talking about creative work. It was suggested that I read Communication Arts and find work that I thought was particularly wonderful or particularly horrifying and then talk to the creative team about creative that wasn't their creative. They'll trust you more if they know you see the world as they do with regard to what we're trying to build as, ultimately, this creative development is an industry of taste.

"If you're not getting what you want, you need a better brief."

Lynette Xanders

EXAMPLE BRIEF: WILD ALCHEMY LOGO

WHAT ARE WE SELLING?

Illumination >> Momentum >> Transformation >> Growth >> Revolution via a Consultation Project

WHAT IS THE ASSIGNMENT?

Create a cohesive and viscerally alluring skin (logo, color palate, fonts) for Wild Alchemy materials that entice people (agencies, clients, individuals) to engage. The set of expressions for the new logo may include a brand book, branded books and dvd covers, presentation materials, website template.

WHY ARE WE DOING IT?

To increase followers, fans and ultimately revenues by 25% YTD. Fill time holes with mailbox money or stuff I can do from PDX. Want more like-minded people (client-friends who believe in quality and allow fun) whether CEO's, creatives or stewards of a company or brand (and its insights and/or communications) — their own or someone else's.

WHO ARE WE TALKING TO?

People with a penchant for elegant solutions, who respect creativity and believe in magic — and who want more (success, fun and magnetism). They are not content with mediocre — in their creative output (outdoor gear to websites) or in their culture. They want to make cool stuff but need a guide.

WHAT DO THEY CURRENTLY THINK?

"I like the basic energy behind this company but the feel is a bit clunky and dated."

WHAT DO THEY NEED TO THINK?

"I have goose bumps. I will find a way to play with Wild Alchemy."

WHAT'S OUR PROMISE?

Mediocrity is death. Let's create something amazing.

WHY SHOULD THEY BELIEVE US?

Wild Alchemy is a creative development whisperer for individuals, companies and agencies. Nearly all client engagements end in a case study that reveals impressive growth results. Engagements with individuals often lead to transformative change. Whether corporate or personal, big or small, local or national, clients leave wildly happy with improved productivity, creativity and happiness (which are inextricably intertwined).

WHAT IS OUR PERSONALITY?

Brilliant + Creative + Fun (think Dr. Seuss + Einstein or Richard Branson).

Old:

New:

“We never seemed to have enough time to do it right, but we always seemed to find time to do it over.”

DDB Head

THANK YOU to all the smart people I've met and worked with who were generous enough to share their wisdoms on this topic. To my clients and creative teams who support me daily in this quest. And to my talented friends who have helped me share this with you. This is a Noble Goal — for the greater good of our collective creative craft.